MW01098379

SHARK
FRENZY

Oceanic Whitetip Sharks

by Thomas K. Adamson

BLASTOFF!
3
READERS

BELLWETHER MEDIA • MINNEAPOLIS, MN

Blastoff! Readers are carefully developed by literacy experts to build reading stamina and move students toward fluency by combining standards-based content with developmentally appropriate text.

Level 1 provides the most support through repetition of high-frequency words, light text, predictable sentence patterns, and strong visual support.

Level 2 offers early readers a bit more challenge through varied sentences, increased text load, and text-supportive special features.

Level 3 advances early-fluent readers toward fluency through increased text load, less reliance on photos, advancing concepts, longer sentences, and more complex special features.

★ **Blastoff! Universe**

Reading Level

Grade **K**

Grades **1–3**

Grade **4**

This edition first published in 2021 by Bellwether Media, Inc.

No part of this publication may be reproduced in whole or in part without written permission of the publisher. For information regarding permission, write to Bellwether Media, Inc., Attention: Permissions Department, 6012 Blue Circle Drive, Minnetonka, MN 55343.

Library of Congress Cataloging-in-Publication Data

Names: Adamson, Thomas K., 1970- author.
Title: Oceanic whitetip sharks / by Thomas K. Adamson.
Description: Minneapolis : Bellwether Media, [2021] | Series: Blastoff! Readers: Shark frenzy | Includes bibliographical references and index. | Audience: Ages 5-8 | Audience: Grades 2-3 | Summary: "Simple text and full-color photography introduce beginning readers to oceanic whitetip sharks. Developed by literacy experts for students in kindergarten through third grade"-Provided by publisher.
Identifiers: LCCN 2020001630 (print) | LCCN 2020001631 (ebook) | ISBN 9781644872482 (library binding) | ISBN 9781681037110 (ebook)
Subjects: LCSH: Oceanic whitetip shark–Juvenile literature.
Classification: LCC QL638.95.C3 A335 2021 (print) | LCC QL638.95.C3 (ebook) | DDC 597.3/4-dc23
LC record available at https://lccn.loc.gov/2020001630
LC ebook record available at https://lccn.loc.gov/2020001631

Text copyright © 2021 by Bellwether Media, Inc. BLASTOFF! READERS and associated logos are trademarks and/or registered trademarks of Bellwether Media, Inc.

Editor: Rebecca Sabelko   Designer: Kathleen Petelinsek

Printed in the United States of America, North Mankato, MN.

Table of Contents

What Are Oceanic Whitetip Sharks?

Oceanic whitetip sharks are large ocean **predators**. They are named for the white tips on their rounded fins.

These hunters live in oceans all over the world. They swim far offshore in the open ocean.

Oceanic Whitetip Shark Range

N
W
E
S

range =

Oceanic whitetip populations are falling quickly. The sharks are in danger from overfishing. They also get caught in fishing nets.

Whitetips are often caught for their fins. The United States does not allow **finning**. But more needs to be done around the world to save these sharks.

Just Keep Swimming

Oceanic whitetips have large, heavy bodies that reach 13 feet (4 meters) long. Rounded **dorsal fins** stick up from their backs.

Shark Sizes

average human oceanic whitetip shark

- - • 6 feet (2 meters) long

up to 13 feet (4 meters) long

dorsal fin

pectoral
fin

They have long **pectoral fins**.
These fins are shaped like paddles.
The sharks use their fins to glide
easily through the water.

gills

Oceanic whitetips must swim to breathe. They swim with their mouths open. Water flows into their mouths and across their **gills**.

Oceanic whitetips have mouths full of triangle-shaped teeth. Each tooth is **serrated**. This helps the sharks make deadly bites!

Identify an Oceanic Whitetip Shark

white tips on fins

gills

paddle-like pectoral fins

Whitetip sharks are not picky eaters. They make meals of squids, fish, and stingrays. Sometimes they even eat garbage!

12

Whitetips may **lurk** near shipwrecks. They are known to attack people who have fallen into the water.

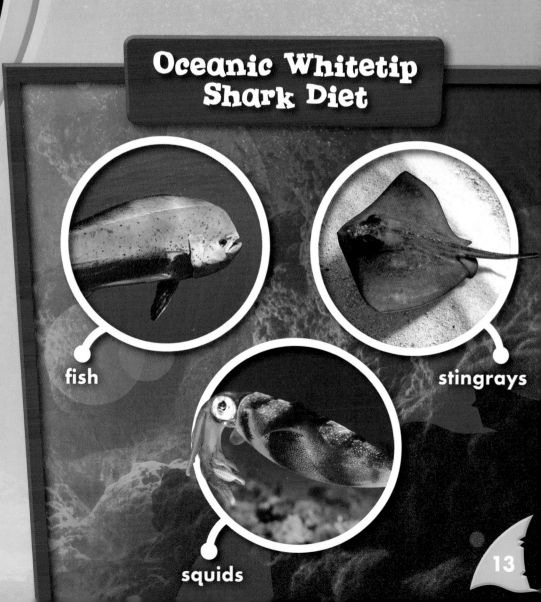

Oceanic Whitetip Shark Diet

fish

stingrays

squids

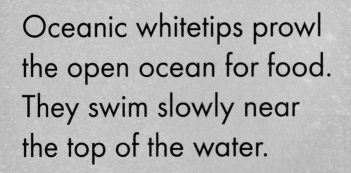

Oceanic whitetips prowl
the open ocean for food.
They swim slowly near
the top of the water.

oceanic
whitetip shark
with school of
pilot whales

Sometimes whitetips hide
among **schools** of pilot whales.
This helps the slow-swimming sharks
sneak up on fast-moving fish.

When there is a lot of food, whitetips gather together in a **feeding frenzy**.

These **carnivores** take charge. They get the first bites while other **species** wait their turn.

Large sharks are predators to young whitetips. But adult whitetips have no predators other than people.

The sharks' low population and open-ocean **habitat** make them hard to study. But scientists are working to help whitetips make a comeback!

Deep Dive on the Oceanic Whitetip Shark

 LIFE SPAN:
up to **22 years**

 LENGTH:
up to **13 feet (4 meters) long**

 WEIGHT:
around **370 pounds (168 kilograms)**

 TOP SPEED:
up to **9 miles (14.5 kilometers) per hour**

 DEPTH RANGE:
at least **500 feet (152 meters)**

white tips on fins

gills

paddle-like pectoral fins

Least Concern	Near Threatened	Vulnerable	Endangered	Critically Endangered	Extinct in the Wild	Extinct

conservation status: critically endangered

21

Glossary

carnivores—animals that only eat meat

dorsal fins—fins at the top of an oceanic whitetip shark's back

feeding frenzy—a group attack on prey by many sharks

finning—removing a shark's fins and returning the rest of the shark to the ocean

gills—parts that help sharks breathe underwater

habitat—the place where an animal lives

lurk—to stay hidden while getting ready to attack

pectoral fins—the fins on the sides of a shark that control a shark's movement

predators—animals that hunt other animals for food

schools—groups of pilot whales

serrated—having a sawlike edge

species—groups of animals or plants that are similar and can reproduce

To Learn More

AT THE LIBRARY

Schuetz, Kari. *Oceanic Whitetip Sharks and Pilot Fish*. Minneapolis, Minn.: Bellwether Media, 2019.

Skerry, Brian. *The Ultimate Book of Sharks: Your Guide to These Fierce and Fantastic Fish*. Washington, D.C.: National Geographic, 2018.

White, Randy Wayne. *Fins*. New York, N.Y.: Roaring Brook Press, 2020.

ON THE WEB

FACTSURFER

Factsurfer.com gives you a safe, fun way to find more information.

1. Go to www.factsurfer.com.

2. Enter "oceanic whitetip sharks" into the search box and click $\mathbb{Q}$.

3. Select your book cover to see a list of related content.

Index

The images in this book are reproduced through the courtesy of: Lukas Walter, front cover; NaluPhoto, pp. 3, 11; Sail Far Dive Deep, pp. 4-5; James R.D. Scott/ Getty, p. 6; National Geographic Image Collection/ Alamy, pp. 7, 14; imageBROKER/ Alamy, pp. 8-9, 11 (gills), 19, 21; Andy Mann/ Getty, p. 10; Stocktrek Images, Inc./ Alamy, pp. 12-13; Beth Swanson, p. 13 (fish); Re Metau, p. 13 (stingrays); Laura Dinraths, p. 13 (squids); David Fleetham/ Alamy, p. 14; David Fleetham/ Nature Picture Library, p. 16 (inset); Brain J. Skerry/ National Geographic, pp. 16-17; Helmut Corneili/ Alamy, pp. 18-19, 21 (gills); Dray van Beeck, p. 22.